GW00870149

NICOLA LEIGH

ALBERT ROSS
THE ALBATROSS

Blue Spaghetti

Illustrated by Lucy, Nina & Luke Howard

Cover by Nicola Leigh

Independently Published on Amazon 2018

Liverpool, England, United Kingdom

Copyright © Nicola Leigh 2018

ALBERT ROSS THE ALBATROSS

BLUE SPAGHETTI

ISBN: 9781976871283

Story by Nicola Leigh

Cover Illustration by Nicola Leigh ©

Inner illustrations by Luke, Nina and Lucy Howard ©

For The Oceans

With thanks to

Luke Howard and Chris Jordan for their
inspiration

...

This is a story about Albert Ross

He is a massive Albatross

Albert's wings are the widest on the planet

and his belly is much larger than a robin's or gannet's

He's too big for his boots

He's too big for his chair

He's too big for his suits

And his underwear!

His jumbo wings mean only he can fly
out to the Deep Spot where red fish swim by

His deep belly means only he can scoop
out enough fish for a huge red soup

So one windy day, when he was out fishing
no red fish, could be spotted out swimming

New food had arrived that was all blue and
stringy

He scooped it up to try, and named it "Blue
Spaghetti"

He flew on home feeling like a winner

Ready to share this new blue dinner

But the birds hated their new blue soup

It was chewy! And sloppy!

And smelled like poop!

"Bird brain, we're starving – this is not funny"
"You've made us angry

and upset our tummies!"

"There were no fish at the Deep Spot, I'm
sorry!

All I saw there was just Blue Spaghetti!"

"Fly further Albert!

Use those big wings, we are hungry!

And you'd better be back here by breakfast,
sonny!"

They shouted at Albert... "We want **real** fish!"

And they kicked him off the jetty!

After hours of flapping and flying about
he felt like a rest as he was worn out!

He spotted a rock, a perfect place for a doze

But wait...
this rock here has some ... toes!?

"'Ello mate!" said the rock, as he sat on its
nose

"Crikey I'm sorry! I've sat on your head!
Are you okay, Mr Turtle?" Albert Ross said.

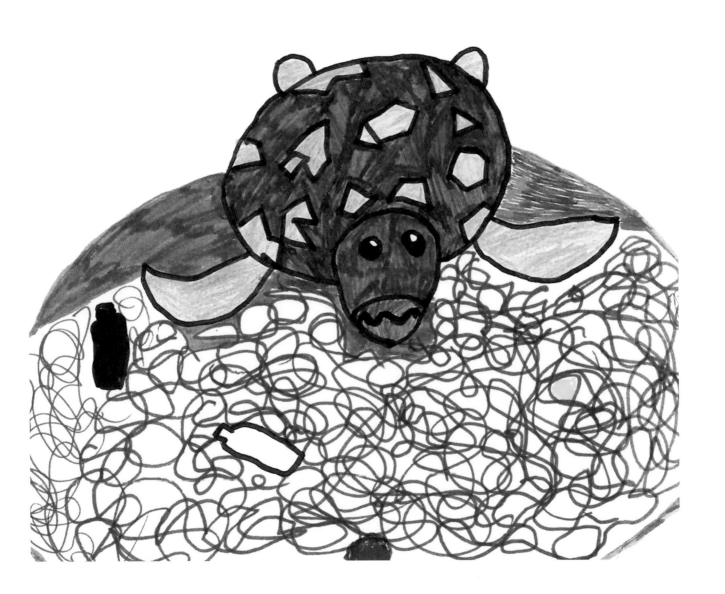

"Oh shucks big bird, please do call me Hugh!
Mr Turtle's my Granddad – I'm only 42!"

"Why are you upside down in the ocean
alone?"

"Well, I'm a bit stuck you see pal...
And I don't like to moan"

"You're all tangled up in stringy Blue
Spaghetti! Can I use my beak to cut you
free?!"

"Yeah thanks, I am in a right tangle, eh?

That is no "Blue Spaghetti" though, let me
explain..."

I thought it was seaweed,
but it's plastic that is!

There's a stinking messy blob down there,
and I'm attached to it

The red fish are scared of it
and have swam to bottom to hide

That's why I am floating here
waiting to be untied!"

"Plastic you say?! No way! That's not right...

We birds just ate that for dinner last night

...though they hated it,

and said it tastes like ducks' feet....

I just couldn't see any red fish left to eat!

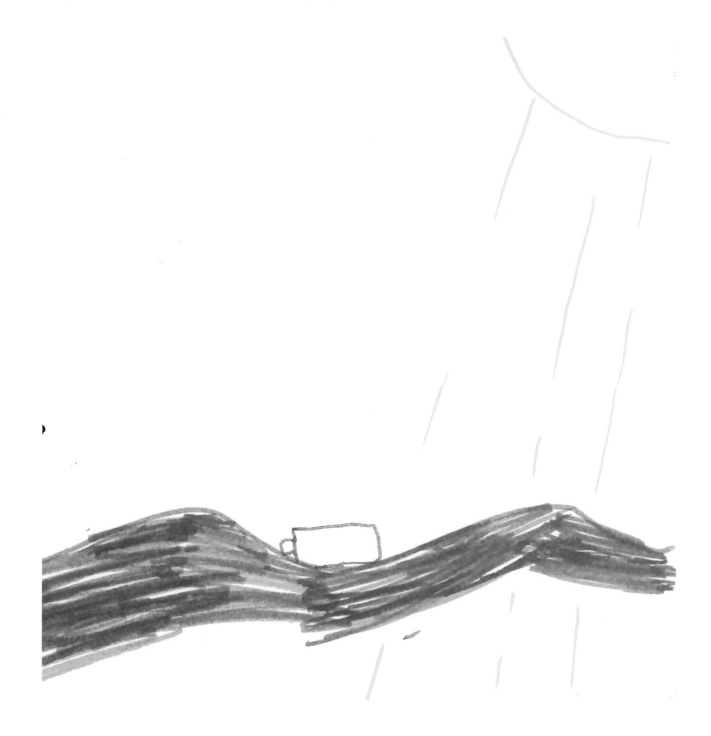

"You birds didn't eat it?!

Oh mate, you can't eat *plastic*

not even *humans* can eat rubber or elastic

it makes everyone who eats it get sick

    – it's real tragic"

"My poor friends – I've got to tell them!

Thanks Hugh, you're fantastic!"

"Mr Turtle, now that your flipper is free...

... would you have time to come and help me?"

"Cheers pal, of course! I owe you my life!

Do I have time to check with the wife?"

"You go and ask her, first I'm going to the bottom..."

"Oh I wouldn't Albert! Down there is pretty rotten!"

"I've got to catch fish here,

the Deep Spot is bare"

"Albert, you're crazy...

Can't you look elsewhere?!"

"No, this is the only spot left with food that's
not blue

I need real fish from the bottom for my
seafood stew!"

Diving deeper and deeper,
into the garbage alone
Albert saw so much plastic
that it made him moan

He saw plastic toys, plastic bags, plastic
straws, plastic goggles,
plastic cups, plastic yoghurt pots
and heaps of plastic bottles

He saw a worried whale,
a sad sea lion, an octopus in a fishing net,
a crazed crab, a sick snail,
and a dolphin with junk 'round her neck

Albert knew he could help them

all from this danger

He's a fisherman after all,

and it's in his nature,

to catch them

and free them, and carry their weight

in his huge tummy to save them...

before it's too late!

SNIP

He freed a worried whale from a spaghetti gag

SNAP

He freed a sad sea lion from a plastic bag

SWISH

He freed an octopus with a swift grab

SWASH

He swiped a toxic bottle from a hermit crab

CLIP

He freed a sick snail from a plastic sheet

CLUNK

He freed a depressed dolphin from a toilet seat

Safe in Albert's belly,

the animals were as happy as can be

They all had big smiles

as he spat them on the sea!

"Thanks for saving us – you're a really nice guy Thank goodness your tummy's as wide as the sky!"

"Guys, we need to clean up that mess

– and I have an idea!

If we all come together

we can make the sea clear

Let's get the birds from my Island, it's not far - quite near"

"We can help you Albert, have no fear!"

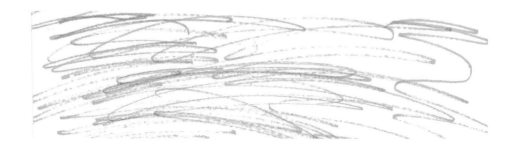

"All right you lazy lot,

I'm back home with news!

If you want dinner

then there's no time to snooze

You see, Blue Spaghetti

is really just smelly old plastic

from a huge messy blob making animals sick

The red fish are scared of it,

and have sank to the bottom

so we need to clean it all up

and fix this problem!"

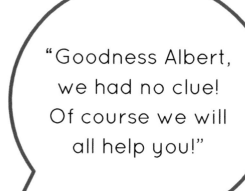

"Goodness Albert, we had no clue! Of course we will all help you!"

"Gobble as much as you can
and we'll fill up my nest
Let's put those albatross wings
to the test!"

"Ready everyone – I'll count to five!

DIVE

DIVE

DIVE!"

"Well done guys, my nest is filling up nicely!

Keep going everyone!"

Albert cheered on politely

We've done it!

We've cleaned it!

My nest is all full!

No more plastic for dinner,

this is wonderful!

We've done it!

We've cleaned it!

The fish are no longer scared!

They are back at the Deep Spot

– I'll get a feast prepared!

HOMEWORK:

We birds and animals cleaned up the trash –
now we have a few question to ask:

Could you please help us and use less plastic?
It ends up in the sea and this makes us sick,
both you and me.

How about bringing your own bags
when you go to the store?

Maybe by clearing up litter from by the
seashore?

How about eating food that's not all wrapped up?

Or trying to use real and not plastic cups?

Could you leave plastic bottles and drink water from taps?

And try to recycle your bottle caps?

We know it's not easy and can't always be done, and we know it is only your decision

But see, we're just birds after all
and even I am quite small

We animals share this planet with you
And you see, this story here is really *true!*

Soon no birds on my island could be left around here
Because more of us die year after year

One day, there might not be enough of us left to breed
And that means the end of albatross birds...

Guaranteed.

ABOUT THE BOOK:

This book came from a spelling mistake.

I was lucky enough to live with the Howard family as an au pair whilst travelling around New Zealand in 2014. I cared for Lucy and Nina, twins then aged 7, and their big brother Luke, aged 9. He loves albatross birds, he always talks about them, watches videos on the internet about them and draws them whenever he can.

Doing homework one night about his favourite subject, the albatross, Luke asked me how to spell the word. Tired from a hard day I got it wrong and said:

"A-L-B-E-R-T-R-O-S-S. Like a name Albert Ross." We laughed at my mistake and also at this new character we could write about for homework.

Luke had to make a book and tell the class about this favourite animal but I felt I had to show him what I knew about what was really happening to some albatross birds – and it was not happy news.

This is a picture Luke did based on a photo taken by a filmmaker called Chris Jordan of an albatross bird on an island called Midway Island.

It's tummy is filled with different bits of plastic, like in the story.

Lots and lots of birds eat plastic accidentally for their dinner and when they do they get sick and don't get better.

I am very interested in how humans use and waste plastic and I try to live without using plastic. This is because among other reasons **plastic can only be recycled once**, and after that it often ends up in the sea.

Old plastic fishing nets (blue spaghetti) can float around and tie up animals, or they eat little plastic bits thinking it's dinner, like in the picture.

I told Luke about this, and he was sad but wanted to help. I asked him how we could fix the problem. He said "Make a giant nest, scoop up all the plastic and melt it down and roll it out with a giant rolling pin"- and thats is where this story started and where my plastic free life began.

Sisters, Lucy and Nina love to draw and have done most of the pictures in this book. They hope that you like them.

Thank you to the Howard family, including Mum Megan, for changing my life and for being such a great plastic fighting team.

   — Nicola Leigh.

Printed in Great Britain
by Amazon